Music

Hanky Panky

And

Family Ties

W E Cameron

Published by New Generation Publishing in 2021

First Edition

ISBN 978-1-80369-023-0

www.newgeneration-publishing.com

FOREWORD

After many discussions over my experiences as a musician over the years, I was encouraged to write this brief but in depth autobiographical look at the many and varied events that shaped my life as a member of a large working class rural family from Perthshire who struggled through the years with a hard drinking father and many family tragedies etc. My intention is to relay the many wee stories that will hopefully give the reader an interesting insight into the social changes that shaped life for myself and my family from the war years to the present day in a light hearted sort of way so please enjoy.

I should mention that the entire family have helped sponsor the start of publication and I am indebted to their response in these difficult financial times. It is heart-warming, so thank you all. Finally, my absolute gratitude extends to my good pal John Ferguson who has helped me get all the manuscript into the accepted format for publication. A true gentleman.

W. E. CAMERON 2021

Chapter 1

Ancestors, parents and family

I come from a long line of Cameron's who were settled in and around the Dunkeld and Blair Athol area of north west Perthshire in the mid to late 18th century. (Probably as a result of dissenting members of the clan during the 45 rebellion) they were all mainly crofters and farmers and settled in a small hamlet called Tomgarrow west of Birnam (now obsolete).

DAD'S FAMILY

Having been born and raised on a farm called Hill of Kinglands between Bankfoot and Logiealmond in Perthshire. Dad then moved to greenfield farm near little Glenshee in the district of Logiealmond serving his time as a stone mason/builder. He met my mother who lived with her widowed mother in the village of Harrietfield about 6 miles from him. His father John Cameron married Mary Graham Easson (my late granny and grandad). My mum and dad got married on 10th of October 1939 in the picturesque parish church at Harrietfield and settled at lower Chapelhill about 3 miles east of Harrietfield. (The Earl of Mansfield's estate.) So, William Easson Cameron and Marguerite Marshall Laing started their life together but of course dad went to war around 1942. My oldest sister and first born arrived in this world on 26/12/39 (Mary Easson Cameron) then along came John

Stalker Cameron on 29/06/41 Then Christina Miller Cameron on 19/01/43

Dad obviously made sure mum had something to do when he was away. My god he was not hanging about and I was born after the war as William Easson Cameron on 06/10/46. We were still living at lower Chapelhill which is situated on a plateau of fields and wee cottages. My elder sisters and brother john joining the primary school at Logiealmond 3 miles west towards Harrietfield. Of course walking to and from school.

My father got a position with Kaey of Methven builders and then moved to Beveridge Builders Perth. I know my mum did dressmaking and was a wizard on her Singer treadle sewing machine and most of our clothes were hand made then handed down where appropriate. It must have been hard for working class families during and after the war although rural families got milk eggs and potatoes from local farms plus rabbits and more than the odd salmon poached from the river almond (illegally of course). Younger brother James Marshall Cameron was born also at Lower Chapelhill on 04/03 /49. We all got stuck into seasonal work when old enough picking berries and potatoes etc. and our mother, despite her condition, grafted hard in the fields as well. A truly remarkable woman.

I must mention the year 1947 when around February, there was a huge snowstorm lasting through to April and all the workmen were off work and digging their way opening up the roads and I remember my father telling me the drifts in places were up near the tops of telegraph poles. It must have been hard on families although the Labour Government started introducing Family Allowance (1948) which at least helped keep families in food etc. during harder times which were often in those days. Around 1949/1950 we moved further down the road a mile or two towards Methven to a farm cottage at Millhaugh (pronounced Mill (hoch), a well-known farm on Mansfield Estates run by Willie Patullo who became a poaching buddy of my dad's and I believe they had many a dram together. I think my interest in music started around the early fifties as my uncle John, my mum's brother, used to call down at the week end for a wee party and a few drams and play his accordion and I seemingly became fascinated with the instrument opening a book and making buttons out of dough when mum was baking and sticking them on to the pages to simulate the accordion. It was always interesting to watch my mother gauge the heat of the oven by inserting her hand into it, (a skill of its own obviously handed down).

Around 1948 I developed double pneumonia and my uncle John went all the way down to Methven in a snowstorm to get penicillin which saved my life. Thank goodness for the recently formed N.H.S.

Life was simple at that time and people were contented with their social gatherings etc and local dances in the village halls which seemed to be more than enough entertainment to keep them happy enough. (a far cry from today, where internet and mobile phones etc have killed the art of social intercourse, especially amongst the youth).

The only down side to living in the countryside was most people lived in "tied" houses and cottages which gave them very little leeway when trying to negotiate repairs etc. It's actually amazing to think that as the monied gentry were steadily coining in rents, the state of some of their properties was appalling. Of course, demand leaned very much in favour of the landlords and always has done even in some cases to this day among urban dwellers. Things changed after the war with a massive council housing development instigated by the newly formed Labour government. This had a bearing on our family as you will see.

Chapter 2

Learning to be resourceful.

Dad earned extra money by setting snares for rabbits (illegally) and he also kept ferrets (which mum detested). We soon learned to catch salmon and seatrout which came up the streams (burns) to spawn using all sorts of methods including torchlight and "gaff" which was a telescopic metal piece with a large hook, easily hidden down the wellies. Although we were cautioned a few times, the water bailiffs were, I think, turning a blind eye as we were eating most of what we caught.

While at Millhaugh, the family increased even further and more siblings came along namely, Marguerite Marshall Cameron 23/07/50 followed by George Robertson Cameron 15/08/ 51 and then Elizabeth Ann Cameron on 06/11/52. Actually, growing up I can recall mum waddling around heavily pregnant. After the war there was a massive building of new council houses (referred to today I suppose as social housing) and the family moved down to Almondbank near Perth to a brand new 3 bedroomed council house at 38 Gellyburn Road. This was around 1953 which of course was the coronation year of Queen Elizabeth the Second. Celebrations were held in June that year all over the U.K. And I recall we went to this down at the Almond Valley playing field at the Perth side of Almondbank village. We all got a coronation mug (I wander how many of these are still in vogue). It stuck in my memory there was a group playing on stage and I was fascinated and wanted to be a musician from that point. Our father was a very heavy drinker and was starting to show violence towards my mother but we managed to cope to begin with at least. Tragedy hit the family when my elder brother john was drowned in the river almond in June of 1955. He had taken my sister Margaret round to a popular deep pool called the black hole. She must have been traumatised to see Johnny lying on the bottom of the pool and rushed home to raise the alarm. He sadly died in the ambulance. We were all at school when we were told and it was unbearable at the time for the whole family.

He was laid to rest in Chapelhill cemetery where our family lair is. John was an exemplary behaved boy and much liked and loved in the community.

Worth mentioning that john on an earlier occasion thought he had a premonition about drowning which is quite scary as mum often talked about it after the tragedy but we didn't like hearing about it. I'm sure he would not mind this next wee story. Obviously, being brothers, we had our fall outs and if dad got to hear about it he would make us put on boxing gloves and formed a ring around the clothes poles at the rear of the house. I always got a hiding as Johnny was older and stronger than me, so I put a stone inside an old sock and hid it behind the pole, where the grass was a bit longer, and when the next situation arose I whacked him on the head with it. He required stitches so mum put a stop to this barbarity. Really. In a sense I won (although I cheated, survival the name of the game).

Another time I got really sorted out by our older sister Mary. Electric coin meters were all the rage in the early to late fifties and when they were emptied, they always handed back a whack of shilling pieces. Mum had laid out all the leftover coins on a shelf so I thought if I take 3 from each heap, she would never know. My mistake was, I came home from the shops with loads of sweets and lemonade etc. and my sister Mary took all the stuff off me and shared it out as she was looking after us when mum was away doing something else. Well, I got a thrashing that night from my dad and put to bed I was never tempted to do it again.

The final two siblings were born at Gellyburn Road, namely Colin Marshall Cameron on 17/09/54. and Adrian Charles Cameron on 20/08/56. Now totalling 10 (9 After losing John), a really big family indeed. During the fifties dad was drinking heavily at weekends and spending the money usually used for food etc. and mum was becoming very stressed and it was advised we go into a children's home near the village of Dunning called Kippen House and that was a horrific experience for us as you will read later.

Chapter 3

Our times at Gellyburn Road as children growing up.

Most of us were at the primary school but of course Mary and Christina (Chrissie) left school at 15 and started to work. Chrissie was a favourite of a certain Mrs Cormack who had a television and we all got to watch children's hour, gathering at her gate and marching at single file to watch programmes like The Lone Ranger, the Sisco Kid and others. We thought this was great and she always had a sweetie for us but Chrissie was her absolute pet.!!! I will always remember Chrissie buying a bike called the" pink witch" and we had to make do with old worn bikes from the war etc. so we tried to scratch it whenever we could (wicked). Although Chrissie was a wee bit spoiled, she never forgot her roots or her siblings. Offering a helping hand and really saving the day when my younger sister Margaret was really struggling with three young children. Chrissie and Robbie her husband really supported the family members who were finding life difficult. This was of course in later years.

The rest of us had a happy and contented up bringing and even at Christmas time mum had limited finance but always managed to give us something and we all learned to appreciate her valiant efforts to create something nice for us all. I think big families support each other and if it came to the crunch, we would look after and protect our brothers and sisters when necessary.

I went fishing with dad on many occasions and we sometimes stayed out all night at places like the underside of the “black bridge at Almondbank for sea trout coming inland from the river Tay. We talked sometimes about the war but he got quite easily upset as I think he had some really horrific experiences as did all soldiers on the front line. When I met with some of dads army friends I was aware that their heavy drinking after the war was probably due to mental issues and of course, same as the present day there is not enough support for ex-military veterans I know this is no excuse for violent behaviour through drink, but it could be a significant factor.

Emergency children’s home

I think my mother did not expect to have any more children after Colin so when this happened you can well imagine the anguish mother was going through and really for her mental and physical health it was decided that 7 of us be put in a children’s home to help mum have the birth and ease the burden for a few weeks.
The home was above the village of Dunning in south west Perthshire and it was called Kippen House. We realised on the first day our stay there was going to be a challenge and I will never ever forget what they put me through. Of course, the Matron called the shots but the carers were to say the least quite wicked as well.

On one occasion at dinner, I was given macaroni cheese which I could not eat as I did not like it so I politely asked for something else. Well, this carer tied my hands behind my back and they force fed me until I was sick with macaroni cheese I was then put to bed and through the trauma of all this I wet the bed and then they thrashed me with a belt across my legs and rubbed my face in the sheets. Because of the worry it would have caused mum we did not tell her and just left it there. Nowadays this would constitute a serious criminal offence. Needless to say, I have never eaten macaroni cheese in my life. Abuse still goes on to this day in these homes. It is a scandal.

On returning home a few weeks later we soon realised mum was struggling with dads drinking but we had now a little brother called Adrian whom I referred to earlier. Mum decided enough was enough and we moved secretly one day on a well-planned operation with the help of my uncle John (my mother's brother) who drove a lorry to a house called Castlemalloch up at Logiealmond where we stayed in the bottom half and Uncle John and Auntie Bet lived in the top. At this point I renewed my keen interest in music and got to play my uncle Johns accordion. We were keen listeners to radio Luxembourg in those days as many Brits were around that time. I was keen to sing popular songs especially Elvis Presley stuff.

Chapter 4

(Little schemes that went wrong!) late 1950's, early 1960's

Dad and Mum made up and the whole family moved down to a house called Cotterton Cottage which was owned by Lumsden Mackenzie mills where dad worked. This was just outside the village of Pitcairngreen up the road from Almondbank. We loved this location as it was a house that sat on its own at the edge of a wood. (perfect for poaching) This was when my dad got me a Hohner Black Dot double row button key accordion. I was only ten or eleven at the time and as we could not afford lessons, I self-taught myself as I went along. I sat the 11 plus exam at Pitcairn primary school. On achieving an A pass at the 11 plus I joined Methven Junior Secondary school travelling by bus from Almondbank station. (Methven lies between Perth and Crieff.) Dad got me a job on Saturdays beating game for the Earl of Mansfield and we got ten bob for getting soaked crawling through bushes and through woodland to put up pheasants etc. It really was slave labour and I hated it (and the aristocratic people involved). At secondary school I used to love getting an audience around me (especially girls) when I would sing and tell jokes etc. I loved it.

I recall one time at this school when we got P.T. (physical training) the teacher for this subject being a Mr Hutcheson who asked us to lie on our back and put our feet in the air and pretend we were riding a bike. I just lay back and he shouted angrily at me “Cameron, I told you to pretend to ride a bike” to which I replied “I am sir, but I am going downhill, you know, freewheeling”!!! well he lost the head and sent me to the headmaster’s room to be punished with 4 of the belt. The headmasters name was Mr Wilson (“greasy” Wilson to us). He used to get very excited when giving you the belt by getting agitated and blowing little bubbles out his wee mouth. (I’m sure he “got off “on it!!) happy days!!

One time at Cotterton Cottage I made a real bow and arrow and tied my brother James to a tree and fired the arrow at a flat football on his head only to see the arrow going into his jaw and pinning him to the tree. What a hiding I got for that. There was another occasion when I came home late from school as I was in trouble and got detention. Mum had made tatties and mince and she offered a plate to me as it was our tea time and I remember saying to her “I'm fed up eating this stuff and I don’t want it”. Well, out of nowhere a plate of hot tatties and mince hit me square in the face which mum launched at me saying “If you can’t eat it, you can wear it then”. I ran outside screaming at her and I remember the free-range hens were chasing after me picking up the bits falling off my face. Needless to say, I told all this my dad when he got home only to receive a hiding and sent to bed. I don’t think I ever complained again as I was absolutely starving by breakfast the following day.

I know my brothers and sisters were in stitches watching me run into the wood with happy hens belting after me for scraps. (happy happy days!!!)

Chapter 5

Latter years at Cotterton Cottage

My father served in North Africa and then Sienna in Italy during the war and hardly ever wanted to talk about it. Anyway, back to poaching salmon on the Dam Dykes at Almondbank around where Lumsden Mackenzie had large bleachworks employing my sister Mary (and my father as a builder carrying out maintenance work on the many houses they possessed including Cotterton Cottage). We pretended we were getting chestnuts and got the odd lovely fresh run salmon for the pot (and maybe the odd hotel). I was standing on a couple of salmon one day covered over with leaves when up came the bailiff and asked me if I was poaching and I said no we are trying to get chestnuts (we kept a wee heap where you could easily see them). I don't think he really believed me but let it go (a close shave).

I think our mother must have got totally convinced that dad's behaviour was not getting any better so we moved this time up to Harrietfield at Logiealmond to a two-storey house called Stormont House. Although slightly run down it was ok for us and as we were now in our teens (apart from Colin, Elizabeth, Adrian and Margaret and George) it only left myself and James and we were nearing school leaving age.

My interest in singing and playing music was always there with me and I loved to show off my talents at new year parties etc. I knew I wanted a trade like my fathers but the situation we were in as a family dictated that I needed a wage that would at least help feed and clothe my brothers and sisters however small my contribution.

Mum worked at Glenalmond College across the river from Harrietfield eventually getting a job in the kitchen beside Ada Murray the head cook (my mums aunt.) As I have indicated before, we were happy with life and learned early on to support our mother and each other but we were really quite poor although resourceful and somehow managed.

My first job was on a farm 3 miles along the road called Drumharrow and I spent the first winter preparing turnips, a process called "shawing" which involved cutting off the leaf part and the roots to leave only the turnip.

This was very hard work but I got a bonus of sorts if I managed to do a considerable amount. My basic wage was £3.17/6d a week and I gave mum £2 of this to help towards running the house. The highlight of my week was a trip down to Perth by bus on Saturdays. I loved when we were on the last bus home and we would start a sing song and I could show off my talent.

My next move was to get a job nearer home and try to get an apprenticeship as a bricklayer but it still eluded me, I think mainly because of where we lived so I took on a job at a farm up the back of the village called Logiealmond Hill run by the Aitchison family.

I was allowed to live in the farm house. It was not long before my family moved down to Scone near Perth to a farm cottage called Newmains. I, by this time took up a position on a hill sheep and arable farm near Aberfeldy called Inchgarth run by a lovely family called McCallum. Donald, his wife Jessie, daughter Catherine and "Lucky" their wee terrier. I was well fed and looked after and passed my driving test in Aberfeldy so this opened things up for me and I became a committee member of the Aberfeldy young farmers and even won Perthshire young farmers speechmaking competition which stood me in good position later on as a front man in the band. I got into the wrong company and started to drink and went through a spell and even left my job at Inchgarth not long after Donald my boss took a very serious heart attack believing I would make much more money just up the road and I know now it was a huge mistake. I eventually moved down to Scone with mum and the rest of the family still left at home.

We soon moved into Brown Street in Perth where I got a start with a civil engineering and construction company called Dreit. I absolutely now felt at home and I also became part of my first band called the Scotstoun Trio consisting of David Batchelor on electric accordion and Andy Rettie on drums (who actually did all the bookings). I was on vocals and started playing guitar (rhythm).

Chapter 6

Getting married and starting a family.

When we were living at Brown Street in Perth, my sister Elizabeth introduced me to the girl I ended up marrying namely, Moragillage Bruce. We got married on 13th September 1969 at the Perth registrar's office. Morag was pregnant and waddled into the Registrars and we all stood in front of this "camp" little man and he just looked at me and asked, "William, do you definitely want to get married?" to which I replied (looking down at her huge "bump") "what fucking choice do I have" creating loads of stifled laughter.

We then went to a nearby hotel and had a good bevvy. It always surprised me how we all just took things in our stride at that age Anyway, we settled down in a lovely residential caravan down the Dundee road at Glencarse village.

Tragedy hit our family once again when my 18-year-old younger brother George was found drowned in the river Tay at a place called Campsie Lynne in the summer of 1970. Things went from really bad to worse when my young nephew Stuart was drowned at Perth harbour in 1974 (he was Christina's youngest). At this point I will tell you that our father was run down by a motorist in the village of Bankfoot in Perthshire and died a few days later. All in all, very difficult to deal with.

At the time we lived at Glencarse, I was working with Beveridge the Builders in Perth and the band was very busy as well. Well, when my dad was killed, he was seemingly drunk at the time which made it really sad as he was a very well-respected tradesman and a true gentleman when sober.

He never really got a proper holiday as we were in tied houses mostly and he had to take his holidays to suit the home farm harvest where he was asked to help as part of the deal with the house (a very unfair arrangement). Meanwhile, Morag and I had 3 children namely Morag born 2nd February 1970 then, Tracy born 7th June 1971 and Lorraine born 14th November 1972.

By this time, we had moved to a two bedroomed house in the Craigie area in Perth (33 Glenlochay Road).

After a couple of years, I was separated from the family and had an arrangement to take them every Sunday and I rarely missed as I was and still am very fond of my girls When I was residing in a flat in South William Street in Perth, I was playing with my band called the Skyliners consisting of myself on guitar and vocals, Mike Jordan on bass and Billy Colburn on drums playing at the Isle of Skye Hotel in Perth as one of the resident bands and we were kept very busy as most bands were in the seventies.

I would like to go back slightly to my exploits with our first band The Scotstoun Trio with Dave Bachelor etc. On many occasions, Dave and I would go to his house out in the country for egg and chips after a gig and one time he realised on the way he had no eggs at home and we decided to steal some from a wee henhouse near to his home. Just as we collected our eggs, we heard a voice calling "who is there" as we could see someone carrying what looked like a shotgun and we dived into a deep ditch and got all stung with nettles and got home eventually with the eggs and a good stiff dram (a close shave).

On another occasion the band had been playing at a dance in the remote village of Kinloch Rannoch when Dave and I got off with a couple of local girls and as we were walking them along the main street Dave was quite drunk and suddenly roared "where the fuck is she"!! He realised the girl's father had snatched her away as they were sauntering along. Dave went back to the band van and I went into the local cemetery and had some fun on a gravestone. I could say she was a "dead cert"!!! ha ha.

During the seventies I got a job as a sales rep. with Singer Sewing Centre in Perth as a sales and service rep after training. I used the van for gigs by altering the mileage etc and had some eventful times to say the least.

I had a spell after that in a music shop in Dundee called Wilkies along with a brilliant musician and arranger called Jimmy Martin. Jimmy played keyboards, and vibes and mainly jazz accordion. He really helped me with my musical career and was a great teacher. I consider myself very lucky to have known him.

Jimmy Martin also did big band arrangements and had a recent spell playing with a big band at the Two Red Shoes in Elgin.

During this time, I met Bill Kemp who was the drummer in Alex Sutherlands TV Band. I also got to know Laurie Hamilton the guitarist with the band who really helped me along and greatly improved my understanding of the instrument. Bill and Laurie had won a jazz trio award along with Jim Mullen in the late fifties. All in all, I met some great musicians and learned a lot from just watching them play and perform.

Also playing around the jazz scene in Aberdeen was the Munce Angus trio consisting of Munce Angus on Piano, Bill Kemp on drums and John Hartley on big bass. They were without question the top modern jazz trio around at the time, especially playing lots of Bill Evans arrangements. The trio were also the backing band for lots of well-known American, Canadian and European jazz giants like Joe Pass, Tal Farlow, James Moody, Eddy Cleanhead Vincen and many others who were guests of the Platform jazz enthusiasts, the volunteer group who brought so many greats to the Scottish scene

Back now to the music shop days for a bit of banter. I recall one occasion where a police driver friend of ours used to spend a fair bit of time with us and became quite familiar. By this I mean he was one day watching me intently marking up the days sales and looking closely at the book asked me "what does music £3.00 zero mean?" to which I replied, "yes, I know what it means but do you know what the initials F. N. P. stand for?" and he replied "no what does it mean?" and I said "Fucking Nosey Parker", which ended the questions there and then with typical musician's humour. While working in Dundee I formed a band still called The Skyliners which consisted of myself on vocal and guitar, Bobby Orobczuk on keyboards and backing vocals, Mike Orobczuk on bass and Billy Foreman on drums who worked with Shirley Bassey and Johnny Patricks band on the T.V. Show the Golden Shot and he really helped us become a slick outfit playing lots of styles like Billy Joel's 52nd street album as well as pop and jazz standards. Eventually we all moved on but we had a really great spell.

I then moved to a position as guitarist and pop vocals with a well-known band from Perth named M.D.Q. Consisting of myself Gordon Esson on clarinet and tenor sax, Jim Webster on lead vocal, Jim Spears on drums and the band leader Jim Muir on keyboards. We played all over but did a regular spot at the Dunblane Hydro with the Jim Mcleod band who were of course resident there and were doing T.V. work as well.

I got lots of gigs from Jim Mcleod and even got a cruise on the P.O. Ship The Canberra. The Mcleod band consisted at that time of Jim on piano and vocals, Alex Doig on drums, Tommy Ford on Accordion and Jim Clelland on keyboards and accordion. We were now well into the eighties and I had lodgings at a house in Methven with Loveina

Fairfull as the landlady whom I befriended and eventually we had a lovely little daughter called Leanne (now my youngest). After a couple of years my debauchery took over and we separated but I saw Leanne every Sunday without fail and I love her to bits to this day. Tragedy hit us again when my younger brother who was in the Royal Navy for some years and who worked in our small building business, died of cancer at the age of 41 leaving a son Christopher and his mother Rona. A terrible loss to us all yet again.

I will mention in this chapter my younger sisters were also married in the seventies. Margaret married Ken Poynter and had 3 children Kevin, Craig and Lucy. Elizabeth married Billy Taylor and had two daughters namely Dawn and Karon. And we all have had some brilliant times and still do.

Chapter 7

At the time I was in the music shop I lived in a wee flat in South William street in Perth and was doing a regular spot at the Moncrieffe Arms next door. This was in the early 80's at the time of the Falklands war and I distinctly remember the announcement one Sunday that the Argies had surrendered and the atmosphere was incredible the whole day after that.

My youngest brother Adrian was in the parachute regiment at that time and I remember the date as being 14th June 1982. A few months after that event I got Alex Sutherlands band to play to raise money to donate to the South Atlantic Fund which was great. I by this time had met a lovely lady called Mary Milne who had a son Andrew and two daughters called Sandra and Fiona but after a couple of years I was tempted by “sins of the flesh” and we drifted apart despite Mary's attempts to help my drinking etc (not good).

My wee daughter Leanne was born on 20th May 1988 but once again I split up from her mum and moved into a flat in St Catherines Court Perth where I took my wee lass on Sundays for tea after a day out. I loved her very much and still do, to this day. I hardly missed one Sunday with her. Our mother died suddenly of a massive heart attack on 13th June 1987 which numbed us all but we retain great memories of her as she was a truly remarkable woman who remained totally dedicated to her family right to the end.

My younger brother James lost his fight with cancer in May 1990 he was only 41. and an ex Royal Navy Sailor. He leaves behind his son Christopher and is very sadly missed as he and I were very close He was a real character and I miss him.

Around this time, I got a call from Fraser Mclellan from Beith in Ayrshire to play with himself and two other musicians to attend the annual Orkney folk festival and I did not know what to expect but got a nice surprise on our first gig They were great players and could really swing with a lively west coast sound which I really liked. They played a lot of Shetland music from the Ron Cooper books which I think set the scene for Scottish (Celtic) style music and modernised the programme.

I was keen to see as many musicians in the bars and halls as I could when we were not playing or taking part in a sit around playing together and furthering our enjoyment of the music etc. I found a lot of really interesting accordion players playing Cajun style or even jazz etc and was really starting to enjoy the whole scene.

There was, for instance a visiting band who claimed to come from Sierra Leone in west Africa playing a fusion of Latin mixed with reggae etc playing steel drums and guitars etc and they were very popular and I seemed to get on well with the band leader. He told me they were really all from the Manchester and Birmingham area, so there we are. Needless to say, I kept the secret.

On one occasion we were booked to play at a concert the BBC were recording and the well-known folk singer and broadcaster Archie Fisher was compering. I was very late and Fraser told me afterwards he was really getting worried as they were on stage ready to begin and I just made it although I tripped over a cable and slightly staggered on stage put on my guitar and Archie Fisher described us in his introduction as like Jimmy Shand on speed. We played a blinder so I was forgiven (I think).

After we got home Fraser asked me if I was interested in a full time place in his band and I immediately accepted and we formed the three-piece ceilidh and mixed Fraser Mclellan Band consisting of Fraser on accordion, myself on guitar/vocals and Jim Collins on drums. Jim had his very own style of playing which I loved as it was lively and slick at the same time and because I was allowed to play my own style using slightly more progressive chords on the Celtic music we developed a very distinct "sound" (Fraser and Jim had played as a two piece before). We really were very busy and I travelled to all the gigs from Perth as we played mainly in the central belt. Fraser and I worked on our programme at every chance we got and I really appreciated his professional approach.

I would like to share a few events that happened during the many years we played together.

Donald and Jessie Mcallum

Catherine (daughter)

Lucky

Dad

Mum

Hill of Kinglands farm

Morag

Left Tracy, Right Lorraine

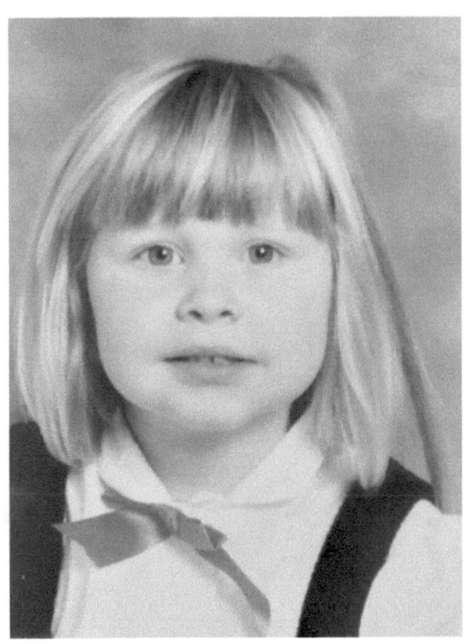

Leanne

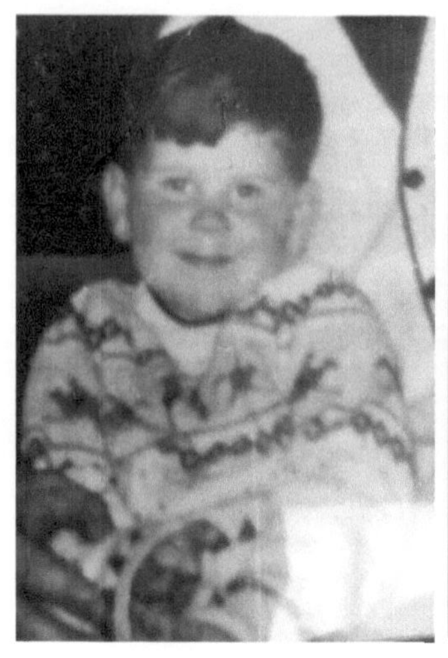

Stuart

brother James

brother George

brother John

Debbie's Wedding

front Elizabeth, Christina, Margaret, Mary
back nephew John, brother Colin, myself, niece Lisa

Next photo is myself and brother Adrian (left to right)

Leanne and Jack

Dale and grandson Jack

Cotterton Cottage

Stormont House

Lower Chapelhill

Castlemalloch

Millhaugh Cottage

38 Gellyburn Road

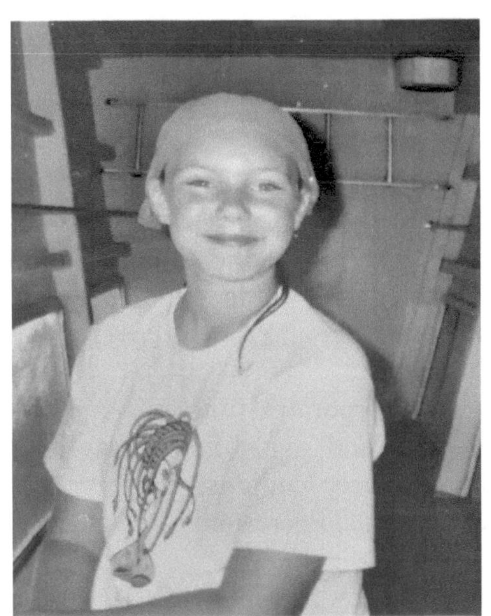

granddaughter Kloe

granddaughter Jade

Chapter 8

Camaraderie and fun in the 90's

We did a regular gig at the famous Renfrew Ferry which attracted a wide audience of ceilidh enthusiasts, often playing for well over 150 people.

As well as corporate functions mainly in the Edinburgh area and gigs like Murrayfield and The Caledonian Brewery ceilidhs. we travelled south of the border on occasions reaching Wales etc.

The highlight of my travels being to Moscow to do a huge burns supper at the Marriot Hotel although with a different line up.

I would like now to draw your attention to a few incidents at gigs etc while with Fraser and Jim.

On one occasion down at R.A.F. Brampton (in John Majors constituency), I thought I would have a wee nose around the grounds and when I reached the perimeter fence, I was suddenly confronted by a very stern looking soldier pointing a weapon at me and marching me back to the guardhouse where they, at my request, got in touch with someone who was organising the event (a wedding). I was released, shaken but not harmed and very embarrassed (never stray on a military base.)

On another gig down south at one of Frasers relatives

where we got a room each with a shared bathroom and I was brushing my teeth, Jim Collins burst in and threw his false teeth into the sink saying, "clean them while you're at it Wullie". Well, I fled out of there with only a towel round me screaming (I cannot abide being anywhere near false teeth and they of course knew this). Fraser once asked me if I would go down to Beith to the family home and go over the roof to check the slates and fix some guttering at the rear of the house. When I replied in my usual manner "Nae problem son". Well, I climbed up the ladder on the 2-storey house and up on to the valley in the roof and made my way up to the ridge where I climbed over only to lose my footing and slid down towards the guttering at the front of the house and luckily managed to stop myself just in time. As I scrambled back up to the ridge and peered over, I looked down to see Fraser and his mum and dad looking very relieved to see me. I actually heard one of them say "does Wulllie really know what he is doing?"

After checking the slates over I got back down the ladder and later we tackled the guttering at the rear of the house which was leaking. We went to the local builders merchant and got the various pieces required. I then stripped down the faulty bits and fitted the new ones and I recall Fraser and his dad saying it all looks very complex and I said "its nae problem lads lets now test it all out with a bucket of water"!! I went up the ladder and poured the water down the valley and when it reached the gutter it burst out all over the place nearly soaking Fraser and his mum and dad. I blamed it on my hangover. A great talking point since, as you can imagine. Needless to say, I refitted the parts properly (Good fun at the time).

The camaraderie in the band was fantastic to say the least and I would not have missed it for the world. I mentioned earlier about visiting Moscow to do a Burns Night at the Marriot hotel and on arrival the manager (from Cumbernauld originally)!! said he would give us a guy to take us out to Red Square etc on a sightseeing tour and the reason I mention this is because you needed a written pass to venture out and he was our pass as it were. Once he stopped to tie his laces and I noticed the huge butt of a gun hidden under his jacket which kind of made us "respect" him even more.

It was a very enjoyable stay, on another occasion, we were taken to this topless night club and treated like royalty with our "bodyguard" alongside us of course.

The piper who was with us was from Forfar had a wife and young child and said he would not indulge in any "frivolity !!" after watching me canoodling with a topless young beauty sitting on my knee. After a few swift vodka's I looked over to see him almost eating this wee blonde girl. Ah! the power of drink eh!!

I don't want anyone reading this to conclude that all musicians carry on like this when away on tour, just the vast majority!!! My life changed a bit when I was persuaded to move to Dalavich in Argyll by a great musician and friend called Gregor Lowrey.

Late 1980's to 1990's

Around the time I was with Jim Muirs band I met his soon to be son in law none other than the infamous Bob Turner, a great piano and accordion player.

Bob and I hit it off immediately and at a time when I was really down and drinking heavily he and his wife Lesley (Muir) gave me a whole load of building work at their wee cottage on the A9 down at Blackford. Bob bought me a Walkman and some great jazz tapes which I listened to as I worked away. Bob and Lesley really saved me from becoming alcohol dependant as did Jim and Helen Muir who gave me accommodation and work at their farm at Meadowside in Coupar Angus. I was really down and all this kindness saved me without a doubt.

Bob and I did loads of gigs and through him I met another famous accordionist called Gregor Lowrey who lived in the village of Dalavich in Argyll.

We all remained buddies for years although I didn't see Bob much after I moved to Dalavich.

After I let bob see my playlist from my previous band namely M.D.Q., he seemed impressed and we spent many hours going through the list which we used regularly on gigs. We did regular country and western gigs at Foresthills complex near Aberfoyle.

Let me now reflect on the time we went to Tiree to do a 21st birthday with my drummer friend Bill Kemp and Fraser Mclellan on accordion. Well, was a new experience for Fraser to see Bill and I get in about the drink at the bar on the ferry.

Fraser only took the odd drink so he left us to it and we got talking to a young man on the ferry who turned out to be the birthday boy at our gig on Tiree. What a session we had and I think Fraser was a bit concerned that we might blow it but the gig was the following evening and although the drink was flowing, we played a blinder and all was well. Sore heads and relative quiet on the way back on the ferry. Bill and I went on to Water Colour Studios on an island over from the the Corran ferry on the road to Fort William where Bill was doing a recording. All in all, a great, few days away.

Chapter 9

A new life in Dalavich.

I will never forget the first day I arrived at the house in Dalavich village we were met by my immediate neighbours Calum and Irene Mclounnan. Calum asked me if I would like a wee dram. Well, of course I agreed and we had another and another until I decided to get my button key accordion out and have a tune. His wife Irene did not know what was going on as she had gone away for a while. On returning to witness the debauchery, she roared to Calum, "you little Tiree bastard what the hell are you doing to those lovely newcomers coming to our village? Calum just ignored her and we went on to have a real session with not a single item except the accordion removed from my van. Actually Michael (Irene's son), was sharpening a chain saw in their garage and he was so funny when he sang out loud that great song line made famous by Nat King Cole, "there may be trouble ahead etc" made all the funnier because we could not see him. A great start indeed??

We eventually got settled in and sampled the ale etc at the local Dalavich Social Club and food at its restaurant part and the local post office and shop owned by Libby and Gregor. I was giving Gregor a hand before we moved up to the village renovating the schoolhouse just outside the village. This work continued on for quite a while after we arrived in the village.

A few weeks after our arrival at Dalavich, Dave Booth and his partner Moira Clarke also bought a house in the village and Gregor and I soon found out Dave was a great musician and guitarist. I remember Dave asked me if I would do some work on their newly acquired house so I asked Calum if he would help. Well, this proved to be a bit of a session once again and I returned to the job next day with a huge hangover.

I will tell you now of a later event involving Dave when he and I performed a song I wrote about the local committee at the social club.

As we were performing this song one Sunday afternoon at the club itself we were met with real hostility by a group of people possessing what I can only describe as "typical village mentality" not allowing a wee bit of criticism or fun in any way especially from newcomers.

Dave and I went over the loch to Jock Hunters house and stayed the night.

Although there were mass resignations after the "song", things eventually settled down, however, I was surprised at the level of hostility from some people (toys out of the pram and all that), but it all receded with time.

Gregor Lowrey is a very keen fly fisher and I took up the sport under his teaching and I absolutely loved it and still of course do. On one occasion we arrived at the loch about 6 pm and we noticed what looked like a boom microphone arm sticking out towards the water. We soon realised it was a lovely Austrian couple who were travelling through the highlands looking to make a film about local characters etc.

It is obvious we rose to the challenge and arranged to share a "cultural" breakfast next morning where we made them a breakfast and vice versa.

After the food we had a few drams with them before I ranted on about the famous Massacre of Glencoe and we played some tunes we all had quite a bit to drink but I think he preferred that so we would show a bit of character. On looking back some time later at the video we did not disappoint although a slight embarrassment was felt by me especially with the drink effect. I just wonder how many people have watched this over Europe where he intended to sell it. All in all, a good bit of fun. My pal Calum eventually lost a battle against cancer and although like many of us he could be an annoying little bugger at times, he was my pal and certainly a character.

Another event that became really popular was the burns supper Gregor and I arranged for a few years at the club. We always got a capacity crowd and I invariably addressed the haggis and recited Burn's world-famous poem Tam O' Shanter.

My pal Dave Booth and I used to do a Wednesday ceilidh for the cabin visitors and Gregor sat in at times and we then got Winnie Mcnicoll on piano all the way from Appin. Gregor and I also used to play for the senior citizens xmas party all for just a few beers and no fee. I kept this up for a few years. As we did not get much help from anyone else in the club when giving our services, we decided eventually to stop. I still get people asking if the ceilidhs will return (ask the committee !!!).

Chapter 10

I was not very long in Dalavich when, due to my keen interest in fly fishing etc. I was offered the job of warden on loch Awe and the associated waters on the north side (Dalavich side) covering Loch Avich which is just up from Loch Awe behind the village. The organisation was known as the L.A.I.A. Which stands for Loch Awe Improvement Association which along with the Scottish Government policy on fresh water angling meant I had to obtain a warrant card. Years with them and met so many different anglers, mostly nice some not so nice (These waters were known as protected fresh waters).

Wee Calum Mclounnan, my friend and buddy in the village used to, on occasions come fishing with us and he would splash around using a method called bubble and fly and it was intrusive if he was anywhere near us fly fishers and sometimes you would hear him shout things like “The wee man from Tiree five, Wullie (me) and Gregor nothing”!!! I think if he had not been such a friend, he would have been going in for a wee swim!!! All in all, an irksome wee bastard at times.

I had a really rewarding experience when I was asked to do the M.D. For a pantomime down in Taynuilt with 60's music set to the tale Rumplestilskin (Grim Bros' fairy tale). We had to audition the youngsters (including teenagers), for the lead singing parts and I was astounded to find so much local talent which made the job such a pleasure.

I was joined by a lovely piano player called Winnie Mcnicoll from Appin and she was so helpful when it came to researching some of the music which was so diverse with excerpts from Jimi Hendrix to the Beatles, The Animals, Petula Clark, James Bond themes and many more including Motown hits.

We rehearsed for a month or two and the shows were held in the Taynuilt village hall with a sell out on every performance. All in all, a great achievement for everyone taking part. What a great experience.

Dalavich the latter years.

During the last few years at Dalavich I took up martial arts as classes were held in the club hall.

I really enjoyed this activity although it was very much at my own pace. It is strange how things turn out as my friend who stayed with me, became the karate instructor's wife and I'll leave it up to your own imagination to assume what went on there???

Anyway, I know myself how these situations can change lives and I'm not here to judge. I have moved on to a much better place. So, I am happy. I developed a heart condition around August 2007 and eventually ended up in Glasgow Royal Infirmary for a spell where they eventually fitted an I.C.D device into my chest. This is an amazingly clever device which monitors every heartbeat and acts as a Pacemaker as well. It can thump in like an external defibrillator.

Of course, I C D means implantable cardioverter defibrillator which is connected to the heart via wires to monitor and correct unusual heart rhythms.

I will have this along with medication for the rest of my days but I am very glad to have it fitted as it has saved my life twice so far. We get a print out of all heart activity through a link with my telephone socket linked to the hospital. This I do every 3 months.

On a lighter note, I remember one time we were all invited to a summer solstice event organised by a close neighbour and after eating vegetarian food (beans and all sorts of pulses and greens) we were told to hold hands in a circle around the fire in the garden and at a certain time (midnight I think), we were to look happy and skip round the fire. I mean the lady giving the instructions was staring at her laptop so we were not really into this so we decided to all try and fart as we skipped. It was absolutely hilarious and it ended up as usual a great night of merriment. I've avoided Druidic dancing since, ha ha.

I did notice that Venus was just behind the Moon that night as was observed by the Druids all these centuries before. Very interesting.

Conclusion of Dalavich Residence and final comments.

Before I conclude I will tell you about a final couple of events worth mentioning.

One morning around 4 am I got a call to say people were in the water down at Loch Awe village and my help was needed. I immediately grabbed my lifejacket and on my way to the Land Rover I slipped on ice and fell very awkwardly and the pain was excruciating Despite shouting for help it took around half an hour before I was rescued and taken to hospital in Oban to see what was happening with my left leg. They gave me pain killers and a special bandage really to no avail as I ended up down in the Royal at Paisley with what turned out to be a broken patella tendon. I was operated on and kept in until a plaster cast was applied the next day. The operation was to re connect the ligament by way of a gauze or wire etc. They made a great job.

The day I was getting the cast put on I had friends in attendance who visited me to see how I was. I do not like watching things like this so I kept blethering while the nurses applied my plaster.

I was aware that the girls who visited me (from the village) that they kept sniggering now and then and when I finally looked down at my leg, they had applied a bright PINK cast and I realised yet another wind up had taken place. Hilarious as I ended up a week later up on the loch fishing like a one-legged flamingo with a specially adapted covering on the right leg. Everyone there was in stitches. Yet another great light hearted bit of banter in life's rich tapestry.

Because of where Dalavich is situated with loads of holiday cabins etc and of course the breath-taking scenery all around, I got my sister Elizabeth and her family up staying each summer which was great. My wee lass Leanne (now about 14) also visited me with her pals from time to time and Leanne learned to handle a bit of driving on the tracks off the main road which seemed to help when she sat her test later passing first time.

I would finally like to mention that I was involved with the renovation of the school at Dalavich into holiday lets for a lovely family that still remain dear friends namely Carol and Chris Keelan. Also, Carol's mother and father who were overseeing the work.

The Keelan family totalled 2 boys and a wee girl during their stay at the village through the lets for the school facilities I also became great friends with John and Joyce Ferguson from Edinburgh John learning the art of fly fishing with some help from myself and Joyce loved the woodland walks which are famous in the area.

I met so many people during my time at Dalavich. I apologise for not being able in this book to mention them all. A fine legacy of reciting Tam O' Shanter prevails as I still to this day do a regular spot at a lovely charity Burns Supper held in the Waterfront Restaurant in Oban. The charity concerned is a very worthy one called Homestart.

My sincere thanks goes to Gregor Lowrey and David Booth for their support during some dark days near the end of my time at Dalavich. Not to mention the support of many people in the village which all helped me through. My building work was enhanced when I met and did church related repairs under Mr Andrew Rose from Kilchrenan who was a joy to work for and a true gentleman to do business with.

Chapter 11

A new life and love.

Before I finished the preparation work to get the house ready for sale, I met my now partner Christine Stewart from Balloch area down at Loch Lomond and she came to Dalavich regularly to assist me in this work. Without that help I would have had to struggle on as I was also fighting a legal battle to claim my share of the equity on the house at Dalavich. Major work was carried out at the rear of the property involving decking and steps etc and of course repair work at the front porch area and the help I received from my pal Gregor Lowrey who is a brilliant joiner was second to none. I eventually moved down to live at Christine's house in the Vale of Leven as a lodger as her son David still lived there.

Meeting others in Christine's family was a joy including her son David, daughter Emma, brother Alan and his wife Terry, sister Jeannett and her late husband Tom, brother Robert and his wife Margaret and her other brother Peter and finally her dear mother Maggie a sprightly 86 year old (I met Christine's other sister Carol later on).

I even met George Stewart Christine's ex-husband when assisting in the renovation of a wee flat in Alexandria. A fine man is George who definitely has a personality all of his own!!! Christine's mother lived in a complex at Bridge Court in Alexandria. And

I will never forget hearing her singing her favourite song the old French standard called 'Jattendrai' which she sang in French. (amazing). What a lady she was as she recently passed away at the grand old age of 94.

"I very soon realised I had good people around me down here and on hindsight I don't miss the "Village Mentality", (which can be interpreted as you feel) and attitudes are different so it took me a wee while but I now love it here. Close proximity to Glasgow (21 miles), allows us to easily access great concerts, theatre, gigs, etc which we take real advantage of. So far enjoying concerts such as 10 C.C. Who were stunning live with their close harmonies and great musicianship etc. also James Taylor (with a great line up including Steve Gadd on drums as well as the brass section from the Crusaders etc. and artistes like Andrea Bocelli the famous Italian tenor who has the most incredible unique "timber" to his voice. Andre Rieu and his Orchestra. Amongst many others and loads more to come, I hope.

Balloch (continued)

One of the most pleasant situations developed when I renewed my relationship with my friend the piano player Bob Turner who lived in Shotts about an hour's drive from here.

I mentioned Bob earlier and as he had a recording studio, I was able to begin preparing for my CD I had always wanted to do involving some of my musician friends over the years.

When I was at Dalavich I wrote a wee song the lyrics of which were written one hung over morning when I was reflecting back on my failed relationships etc and as it turned out, this was the first one we recorded. The title of the song is Through the Years.

Whilst we were well through the preparation stage for the final take I got a great surprise to learn Bob had arranged for a professional tenor sax player friend from London to do a nice middle 8 solo and it blew me away when I heard it and of course it remains a feature on the final recording.

I also wrote a wee "fun" song about fishing simply called the fishing Song which, in a simple way without being too involved musically, is a wee laugh at our angling days and reflects on a lifetime of trying to catch wild brown trout. Again, Bob did piano and accordion on this one which turned out fine. The chorus is quite catchy and is proving popular with lots of would-be anglers.

I am of course writing all this after we lost Bob to the dreaded COVID 19 which very sadly took him from us all on 17th November 2020.and it makes it all very difficult but I am getting through it ok.

The complete sense of loss here is almost overwhelming but time itself is a great healer although we never lose the memories which are so precious. Bob leaves behind so many friends in the music business and also his son Ben who has autism and Bob just completely adored him. I hope both Ben and his mum Lesley find peace eventually from the many memories they have Bob's lady friend Lesley warrants a special mention here as she was with him at the end and has shown such dignity throughout.

Chapter 12

My ongoing life in the "Vale".

I still travel to Perth to see my family when I can and usually stay at my sister Elizabeth's house in the village of Abernethy. Elizabeth and her husband Billy (Taylor) have two daughters namely Karon and Dawn who both have children and have "flown the nest" as it were but come home now and then so we all get a chance to meet up for a wee drink and a nice meal as my sister "Liz" is a very good cook which is great. Liz likes a drink now and then (every 5 minutes or so actually) ha ha!!

My younger brother Colin also had a house in Abernethy and my youngest daughter Leanne and her partner Dale bought the house when Colin downsized and moved to Perth. Christine and I painted the whole of the inside of the house for Leanne and Dale and they then moved in.

Leanne got pregnant but tragically lost the bairn (a wee girl) with only a few weeks to go. It almost destroyed her but they bravely tried again and she gave birth to a lovely little boy called Jack and he is a wee star. They recently moved to Toronto in Canada and have settled there with Dale's folks at the moment as they already live there. Leanne is a highly qualified hairdresser and is carrying on her business in Canada.

Leanne and Dale are very ambitious and I greatly admire their enthusiasm for life especially after what they have been through and they will do well, I am sure. Leanne is made of stern stuff. Let me now mention my other 3 daughters namely Morag, Tracy, and Lorraine. Morag my eldest lives in Perth and travels daily to a nursing home down in Auchterarder where she works. Tracy has for many years worked with Scottish Power and lives in East Kilbride and Lorraine lives in the village of Balbeggie north of Perth with her husband Paul (Gilzean) and they work very hard and have a lovely bungalow and garden etc. Paul runs his own delivery business and Lorraine works as a carer Lorraine has 2 daughters to her first husband called Kloe and Jade who live elsewhere and have full time occupations. I love them all despite the fact that we don't see them very often I of course, keep in touch.

(Balloch recently)

Bob Turner and myself had played a few gigs around the care homes as a two-piece using backing tracks and live performances where possible. It has taken me all this time to accept the concept of backing tracks for my songs but really if it was good enough for great musicians like the late Lawrie Hamilton then I can totally accept that as long as I can do the guitar parts myself where possible, I am starting to really enjoy it.

Bigger bands are harder to pay and its possible for an experienced musician to easily handle a gig. I have the advantage of being able to play ceilidh music on my accordion as well.

Bob and I also recorded for my forthcoming CD some poetry of the Bard Robert Burns and he was responsible for the very clever “atmosphere” created behind my rendition of the famous Tam O' Shanter with eerie background stuff which makes such a difference to the finished recordings.

I found it difficult to record the poem and give it my best as, without a live audience it takes a wee bit away from it all, however, I am more than happy with the result.

Although it has been 8 years since I left Dalavich village, I still enjoy the camaraderie of meeting up with my pals and my two younger brothers on fishing trips during the summer months This has become a regular trip each month or so and we stay in our tent trailer for a few nights. The banter is great and the competitive spirit around who catches the biggest “brownie” of the day still very much exists and adds to the fun (the fishing song alludes to all of this). So, I’ll play it loud from now on!!!!!

As I mentioned before, my now partner Christine has helped me through all the court case stuff re the equity of the house at Dalavich when it was all going on and of course we won our case at Oban Sheriff Court with the help of a very able solicitor. After things settled down, I think I slowed down a bit and please don’t judge me as a total womanising, heavy drinking debauched musician with scant disregard for the fairer sex. I have simply tried to give an honest appraisal of my experiences to afford a whimsical look at life as a musician over the years.

Chapter 13

Around 2018 onwards we seemed to have a spate of tragedies in the family and I will of course mention them here.

Mary, my eldest sister lost her youngest daughter Alison who after a long battle with drugs etc sadly took her own life in July 2018 (she was only 45 years old). Mary was frail herself and in a nursing home which must have been really hard for her although we all did our best to support her. My sister Mary herself passed away on 2nd October 2019. She was 80 years old. Mary grafted hard all her life as an auxiliary nurse at the nearby Hillside hospital and I think all the very heavy lifting of dead weight patients etc left her joints etc very badly affected. We all love and miss her dearly. As if all this was not enough, my Niece Carol (Christina's daughter) died very suddenly on May 18th 2019. Carol since birth had a very serious condition with fluid on the brain which left her disabled but she went on to have 2 lovely boys Graeme and John who will miss their mum terribly as we all do. She was one very brave and lovely human being but lost the battle in her early fifties So sad. Leanne, my daughter, lost her mum before she became pregnant It was very sudden and Leanne had her own troubles to deal with. As you are aware, Bob Turner was taken with Covid19 which we are all still battling against the world over and I hope now with the vaccine we will soon be living some sort of normal life once again.

I myself have had my first jab and awaiting my second soon I hope. Well, I hope I have given you an insight into the world of William Easson Cameron (myself) who has led an interesting and very varied life thus far and of course I have covered the years and decades from the war years to the present with some lighter moments to ponder and I sincerely hope it has given the reader a good insight into what it has been like for a large rural family living in Perthshire.

Finally, I would like to mention my second cousins Ian and Hamish Cameron who inspired this book after giving me a copy of our family tree etc and I hope to have a wee dram with them soon.

Cheers to all and thank you for reading my first attempt at writing.

W E CAMERON

www.ingramcontent.com/pod-product-compliance
Ingram Content Group UK Ltd.
Pitfield, Milton Keynes, MK11 3LW, UK
UKHW042000190726
13854UKWH00005B/2084

9 781803 690230